BOULLE'S JEWELS

THE BUSINESS OF LIFE

CONTENTS

CREATE COMMAND WORK

LIKE A GOD

LIKE A KING

LIKE A SLAVE

CONSTANTIN BRÂNCUŞI

INTRODUCTION

Countless books have been written about how to maximise your potential, but they all seem to be by people so far over the hill they've practically disappeared from view. With the arrogance of youth, the courage of my convictions and vast experience gleaned from the last twenty-four years, I offer this guide in the hope of inspiring you to create the life you deserve. Be audacious. Be bold. Be me.

Just kidding. Be you, of course. The best version of you that is ... the newly minted, 24K gold, *Boulle's Jewels* version.

Francis Maximilien Yvan Christophe Boulle

MY LIFE FROM ROUGH DIAMOND TO POLISHED GEM

(T MINUS 3 MONTHS)
The as-yet-unborn Baby Boulle conquers Mount Fuji in his mother's womb. This pre-birth feat marks him out as destined for great things.

1 MONTH OLD
Packs nappy bag and moves to Paris, taking family with him.

2 YEARS OLD
Honing his illusory talents, Francis goes missing in The Hall of Mirrors, Palace of Versailles, prompting security lockdown. He emerges from behind mirrored panels, exclaiming, 'Let's buy this house, Daddy.'

8 HOURS OLD
Perennially late, Francis decides to grace Planet Earth with his presence, arriving in his own time on 20 October, three-and-a-half weeks late. Living up to his pre-birth rep, he does his first press-up on Day 1, lifting his upper torso and head to check out the nurses at Queen Charlotte's Hospital. He proves very popular.

6 MONTHS OLD
Francis Maximilien Yvan Christophe Boulle is christened at thirteenth-century church, Église Saint-Etienne, near his Fontainebleau family home whilst his two-year-old cousin, Patrick, repeatedly regales the parishioners with his newly acquired word: 'FUCKER!'

8 YEARS OLD
Like his namesake, Francis of Assisi (and Jesus), Francis 'rescues' a lamb from a flock in the neighbouring field, raises him, tags him and sells him back to the same unsuspecting farmer.

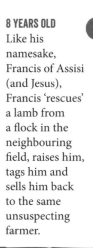

10 YEARS OLD
Inspired to take up polo after seeing his father play at Cowdray Park. Begins practising on his first polo 'pony', a bike named Ozark.

9 YEARS OLD
Watches the *Back to the Future* trilogy more than 100 times and begins to heavily contemplate the philosophy of time. Does not get a DeLorean for Christmas. Builds a cardboard DeLorean in the barn.

3 YEARS OLD
Begins education at l'école maternelle in France, but is sent home on the first day for thumping his classmate, Thibaud.

11 YEARS OLD
Family relocates to Florida where Francis begins honing his surfing and skateboarding skills (see p100). Shreds hard, obviously.

Interviewed by local news for discovering and joining efforts to rescue nine beached pilot whales. Two lived.

16 YEARS OLD
Saves baby wild hare from becoming roadkill, taking it back to school and raising it secretly in the drawer of his dorm-room desk. Charges lower year boys £1 for ten minutes of 'Bunny Cuddles'.

17 YEARS OLD
Gets caught in flagrante in a dormitory with a girl from the nearby girls' boarding school. Reprimanded by both headmasters and the girl's parents ... oh, and her brother.

Were allegations accurate, this would also have been the time Francis purchased 7,000 crickets, beetles and locusts from a live-bait website, releasing them in his school atrium under the cover of darkness. Francis has never confirmed or denied the allegations.

13 YEARS OLD
With sun-bleached blond locks, waterboy Francis returns to the UK and reapplies his stellar water skills to competitive rowing at his new boarding school.

22 YEARS OLD

Returns to London as the media world beckons, providing an ideal platform to promote his new business ventures, as well as his sweet skateboarding skills.

24 YEARS OLD

Publishes first of many international bestselling books.

 = £

18 YEARS OLD

Francis gets through three days of gruelling Oxford interviews and is told by the college that he has finished. Six hours and as many G&Ts later, he is unexpectedly summoned back for another interview with a different college. Reeking of gin, Francis is grilled by a panel of monks and tutors, hiccups and says goodbye to his Oxbridge dreams. The University of Edinburgh beckons.

Reads philosophy at Edinburgh, attends a few lectures and plays even more polo. Sets up an international precious-metals brokerage in his dorm-room. Discovers his Midas touch.

WOLF MAN

Whilst I generally shy away from direct comparisons between myself and greats like Johnny Depp or Winston Churchill, I must concede that we do share a fair bit more than just good looks (Depp) and statesmanship (Churchill). It appears we are also blood brothers, sharing Native American ancestry on our maternal sides.

I descend from the Wolf Clan of the Cherokee Nation, Western Band. My great grandmother was a full-blood Cherokee Indian. For reals.

Incidentally, as a professional athlete, she and her championship team were also inducted into the Basketball Hall of Fame. No visit to her house was complete until she had mercilessly schooled you in a game of backyard hoops.

swish

'LIFE SHOULD BE DRIVEN BY VALUE TRADES – I LEARNED THAT AGED NINE WHEN MY MOTHER FLEECED ME ON A DEAL'

LET YOUR CAREER FIND YOU

DON'T BE AFRAID TO EMBRACE
EVERY EMPLOYMENT OPPORTUNITY
UNTIL YOU FIND THE ONE THAT'S
RIGHT FOR YOU. IT TURNED OUT THAT
UNDERWATER FIREFIGHTING WASN'T
MY LIFE'S WORK...

WHICH BUSINESS

As a consummate strategist, Machiavelli taught us that in war, as in business and life, you must be the lion and the fox simultaneously: combining the intimidation of the lion and the strategy of the fox. Which business animal are you? I've seen them all since I became an entrepreneur. For reference (and it's always useful to have these characteristics in mind when you meet new people), here's a quick profile of the most common business animals.

LION: The leader. You can't have a business without a lion. Lions represent the strength behind the brand and the power behind the organisation. It helps if the CEO also has a formidable mane of Heseltine-like locks.

SNAKE: You can admire snakes, but keep your distance and on no account attempt to do any deals with them. As my Cherokee grandpa says: 'Don't be surprised when a snake turns and bites you in the ass. The snake was always a snake.'

FOX: Every business needs a thinker, someone who knows the territory and can plot the most profitable course through it. If you're a lion, get a fox as a business partner. Better still, be both yourself.

ANIMAL ARE YOU?

MONKEY: I don't really get on with business monkeys: they see business as play, recreation. Business is not for monkeys.

LEMMING: Basically a bureaucrat. There's nothing wrong with that, but a lemming instinctively does things the way they have always been done so it's not suited for riding the high seas of entrepreneurialism.

'THE LION CANNOT PROTECT HIMSELF FROM TRAPS, AND THE FOX CANNOT DEFEND HIMSELF FROM WOLVES. ONE MUST THEREFORE BE A FOX TO RECOGNISE TRAPS, AND A LION TO FRIGHTEN WOLVES'
NICCOLÒ MACHIAVELLI

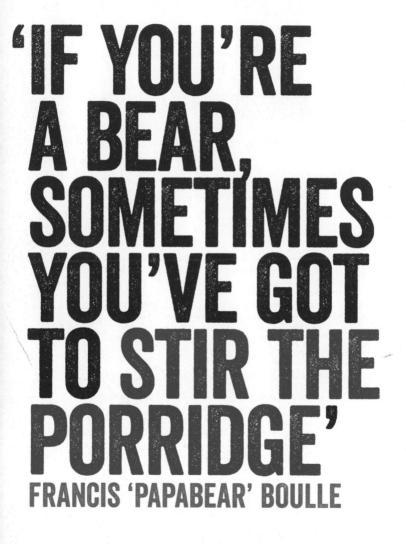

'IF YOU'RE A BEAR, SOMETIMES YOU'VE GOT TO STIR THE PORRIDGE'

FRANCIS 'PAPABEAR' BOULLE

THE EXERCISING OF POWER IS A WELL-KNOWN APHRODISIAC...

...A BIT LIKE DIAMOND MINING AND BEING ABLE TO SKATEBOARD.

IS YOUR MP

Sexy?

THERE ARE NO HARD-AND-FAST RULES ABOUT POLITICAL APPEAL – EVEN SOCIALISTS CAN HAVE A CERTAIN ALLURE, PARTICULARLY AFTER A GLASS OR TWO OF CHAMPAGNE AND A RIVETING IDEOLOGICAL ARGUMENT.

Ask yourself the following questions. If you can answer 'Yes!' then you're probably living in one of the favoured constituencies of SexyMP's Top Ten Tantalising Totties, if you see what I mean.

 When you hear the phrase 'Party Whip', do you think of your MP?

 Likewise the expression 'Climbing the greasy pole'? Does your MP's surgery conjure visions of doctors and nurses?

 When you find out your MP has been claiming for a second property in Barbados/porn films/ enough food and fine wine to feed a Third World state, do you think, 'Well they deserve a little R&R'?

N.B. *That Louise Mensch was pretty cheeky, IMHO.*

Exercise your right to vote at **www.sexymp.co.uk**

'BUSINESS IS WAR... AND I'M THE GENERAL'

FIVE EASY STEPS TO BUILD YOUR EMPIRE

1 BUILD A CAPITAL BASE

2 LAUNCH A COMPANY

3 RE-INVEST

4 EXPAND AND ACQUIRE

5 RINSE AND REPEAT

'ALL THE FORCES IN THE WORLD ARE NOT SO POWERFUL AS AN IDEA WHOSE TIME HAS COME'

VICTOR HUGO

STAFFING THE EMPIRE

- Employees should be clever, ambitious and well–presented.
- They should be a credit to you in public, and always willing to walk three steps behind you.
- They must also be punctual and reliable – only the CEO can be creative with time.
- If they're attractive, put their desk near a window. It will bring in new business and keep the window cleaner keen.
- If they screw up continually, don't be afraid to pull the rip cord.

STAFFING THE EMPIRE

HIREABLE ATTRIBUTES

- Smarter than boss
- Better looking than boss
- Funnier than boss
- Good suit (Savile Row preferable)
- Wears Serge DeNîmes on their day off
- Excels at polo and surfing

FIREABLE ATTRIBUTES

If you want to stay in work – with me or any other decent employer – avoid the following:

- Square-toed shoes
- Novelty cufflinks
- Four-button jackets
- Short-sleeved dress shirts
- Tie tucked into shirt
- Ties that stop at your navel
- Skinny ties
- A tie that matches your shirt
- Fat Double Windsors
- Vest showing
- Anything polyester
- Tracksuits or leather jackets
- Socks that allow even a glimpse of flesh, and white socks with anything other than trainers
- Wearing a ski parka over your suit in winter, or anywhere except on the slopes

WOULD
YOU HIRE
THIS MAN?

'YOU CAN
TELL A LOT
ABOUT A MAN
BY HIS WATCH,
HIS WIFE AND
HIS SHOES'

'IN YEARS TO COME, WHEN PEOPLE LOOK BACK ON THIS, I THINK IT'LL BE CLEAR WHY I'M HOLDING THIS GLOBE'

PRINCIPLES OF ENTERPRISE

'THEY SAY THAT YOUR EVENTUAL NET WORTH WILL BE THE AVERAGE OF YOUR FIVE CLOSEST FRIENDS, SO CHOOSE THEM WISELY'
FRANCIS BOULLE

1 There's no shame in reinventing the wheel. More successful businesses than you'd think are based on a variation of a pre-existing idea. You can emulate an idea but most importantly, you must improve it. Think green ketchup.

2 Start looking at the world through the lens of potential profit: everything you see, every person you meet, every occasion you attend should be an opportunity to make money. Collection basket at church excluded.

3 Remember to feed and water your staff, and reward them with day trips to the zoo.

4 Your competitors don't have to be your enemies – you can learn a lot from them. Just don't let them learn too much about you in the process.

5 Lawyers are good. Contracts essential. Never trust anyone who is prepared to do business on a gentleman's agreement. He might not be a gentleman.

6 Surround yourself with success and intelligence – both are infectious.

7 Agree a price up front and get it in writing. My mother got my first ever invoice after I'd fixed the VCR when I was nine. But we hadn't agreed a price for the job beforehand. She fleeced me on the deal, claiming that my payment was continued food, shelter and lifts to school. A tough, but necessary, life lesson.

8 A good business partnership should be like a good polo player and his horse: the two should have the same goal and complementary, but different, skills.

9 Always have an exit strategy, but keep it legal. Best to exit without handcuffs.

'YOU DON'T GET RICH SPENDING MONEY. SPEND LESS, EARN MORE'

THE HOLY TRINITY OF MONEY MANAGEMENT

SPEND A THIRD

SAVE A THIRD

INVEST A THIRD

THIS CONCEPT WAS ILLUSTRATED BY MY MOTHER WHEN SHE GAVE ME MY FIRST ALLOWANCE AT THE AGE OF FIVE, AND SUBSEQUENTLY TOOK TWO-THIRDS BACK: ONE-THIRD FOR MY PIGGY BANK AND ONE-THIRD TO INVEST IN MY BURGEONING STAMP COLLECTION. CHEERS, MUMSY.

For the grown-up version turn the page...

THE HOLY TRINITY OF MONEY MANAGEMENT

SPENDING

When spending, by all means enjoy your money. However, where possible, buy things that will retain and ideally accumulate asset value.

 GOOD BUYS: wine, vintage watches, art, classic cars … this book.

 AVOID: new cars, expensive perishables, call girls, cheap champagne, peacock farms.

SAVING

As with spending, the key to saving is to protect your asset value and buying power. So when I say save a third, I do not mean just stick one-third of your pay cheque into your bank account and let it sit there. Holding currency not backed by a commodity simply exposes you to the printing presses of the central bank and you will lose buying power.

Hold savings (unleveraged) in a relatively stable asset and something that has traditionally been treated as a store of value. I am a big fan of commodities and precious metals, in particular gold and silver. Find a secure storage facility, ideally a vault on a South Asian volcanic island. It works for me.

INVESTING: BOULLE'S
MARKET PICKS

John Steinbeck astutely remarked: 'The reason Socialism never took hold in America is because the poor there see themselves not as the exploited proletariat, but as temporarily embarrassed millionaires.' It's all about the attitude, kids.

Everyone – no matter how young or old, rich or broke – should invest one-third of their income. When you are still young, you have the advantage of being able to take bigger risks and so for a young person at school or university, or who is newly employed with not much money to play around with, I would recommend starting with micro-cap and penny stocks. The volatility of smaller cap stocks can be exciting and you can make a lot of money very quickly but you can lose a lot of value in your initial investment too, so never invest more than you can afford to lose. The same applies to women, Vegas and Ascot.

Personally, I look out for not only stocks that have a great potential to rise, but also stocks that have the potential to fall and make good shorts. If you are interested in learning more about investing, getting a grip on financial jargon and seeing what companies I am investing in, then subscribe to BoulleMarketPicks.com for my weekly market rundowns and stock picks.

DISCLAIMER: *Should you find yourself continually suffering losses or sleeping in the doorway of the local betting shop, it might be time to call your local chapter of Gamblers Anonymous. Remember it's about SMART money.*

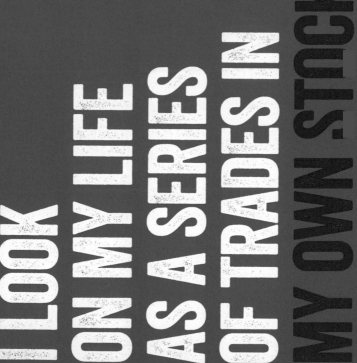

I LOOK
ON MY LIFE
AS A SERIES
OF TRADES IN
MY OWN STOCK MARKET

THE BOULLE INDEX

Like all good stock traders there are times when I'm not sure whether the market will go up or down, so I hedge my life decisions. In other words, I always have a fallback plan in case things go south.

There are so many situations where you can hedge and ultimately win: buying watches, cars, pets or horses, or choosing girlfriends/boyfriends (and fiancées/fiancés – see THE DATING GAME, p60).

In business, always hedge: if you have to break up a partnership or business, do so with as much grace as you can muster. You never know when you might need to work with, or go on holiday with, your ex-partners again.

'LESS TAX, MORE CHARITY'

PAY IT FORWARD

When you're fighting your way to the top, it's all too easy to only look forward. Remember to be alert to opportunities to help others on your way. You never know, you might meet them again on your way back down. Practise random acts of kindness and spread the love. Buy an extra sandwich for the *Big Issue* guy on the corner, audition ~~girls~~ students for work experience, designate someone to be your 'Bro for a Day', or leave your number instead of a tip after a great meal. You get the picture. Do a good turn, particularly to those most in need. (Disgraced bankers and Bernie Madoff do not count…)

IQ. DO YOU?

SURROUND YOURSELF WITH SUCCESS

As the saying goes, success breeds success. Now, this doesn't mean you will only achieve the lofty heights of your ambitions if your father (or mother) forges the way for you. It means that you must seek out opportunities to encounter and observe successful people in your daily life and where you will be constantly stimulated and inspired – like working for me.

Anthropologists and scientists have found (in countless studies) that humans have a natural tendency to mimic the people around them. So, pet chimps aside, surround yourself with those who will have a distinct effect on your habits, your behaviour and therefore your financial destiny.

I've always been drawn towards people who are passionate about leaving a mark on the world, who are smart, hungry, ambitious, creative and charismatic. Not only will you learn from these types, but seeking them out as mentors, friends and business partners will inevitably raise your game. Life should be about expanding your knowledge and awareness as much as expanding your empire. Try to befriend people called Stephen, or any derivative of the name. They seem, proportionately, more successful than the rest of the population.

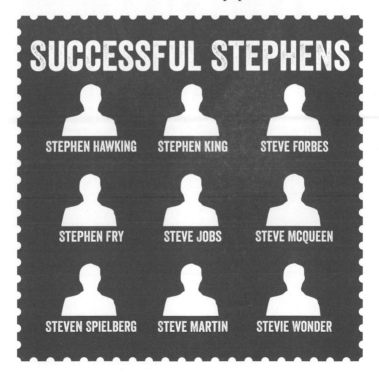

SUCCESSFUL STEPHENS

STEPHEN HAWKING   STEPHEN KING   STEVE FORBES

STEPHEN FRY   STEVE JOBS   STEVE MCQUEEN

STEVEN SPIELBERG   STEVE MARTIN   STEVIE WONDER

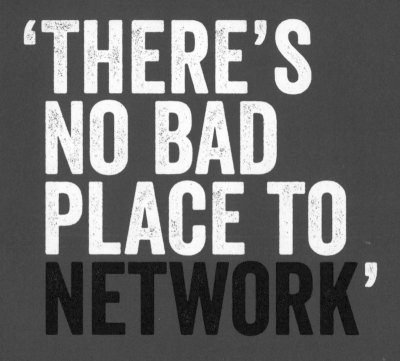

NETWORKING ISN'T A NINE-TO-FIVE ACTIVITY, IT'S A WAY OF LIFE. I NEVER STOP NETWORKING: WHETHER I'M WORKING OUT, SKATEBOARDING, HAVING A PICNIC OR PLAYING POLO – ALMOST EVERYWHERE HAS NETWORK POTENTIAL. MY MOST SUCCESSFUL BUSINESS CONNECTION WAS MADE IN THE SMOKING SECTION OF A CLUB – NOT THAT I ENCOURAGE SMOKING. HERE ARE SOME BOULLEIAN NETWORKING TIPS:

1 Play the long game – allow relationships to grow and mature rather than go for the quick, cynical win.

 5 Have many and diverse interests: your network will be exponentially bigger.

2 Make it clear that you want to do business without coming across as desperate. You don't want to look like a fake-watch hawker.

6 Always carry business cards but remember it's often better to receive than to give: it allows you to dictate when and how to take the next step.

3 Say less than necessary at most of your meetings: it's better to plant seeds than to try to harvest the fruit straight away.

 7 Be discreet and use common sense. Best not to approach anyone at funerals or AA meetings.

4 Let people find out from others how you work and what you do: you're more appealing if you're an enigma.

 8 Generally, it's bad form to network in places of worship, with the exception of banks.

When you introduce two parties who engage in business you can justify taking some brokerage or an introductory fee. In love, when you play matchmaker your remuneration is less tangible and more long-term. If it is a successful match it can come in the form of a wedding invitation. *I fucking love weddings!*

Despite my love of weddings, and the satisfaction I receive in introducing two suitors, what truly gives me a buzz is introducing smart people and companies with bright ideas to the investors who can make those ideas profitable. This is why I founded Fundmine.com, to help bright ideas meet smart money. *I fucking love smart money!*

'IN LOVE AS
IN BUSINESS,
WHEN PLAYING
THE DATING
GAME — YOU'VE
GOT TO WIN AT
ALL STAGES'

THE DATING GAME

PHASE 1: PICKING A GIRLFRIEND

THIS IS WHAT I'VE LEARNED ABOUT DATING SINCE MY FIRST SERIOUS CRUSH, AGED SIX, ON A GIRL IN MY FRENCH CLASS.

GIRLS TO GO FOR: Athletes, ballerinas, yoga teachers, surfers, tennis players. The ones with the healthy yoga glow and supple limbs. They tend to take care of themselves.

GIRLS TO AVOID: Girls working in fashion are tricky. They look good, start with the best intentions but sometimes things go off the rails. That's just my experience and I'd love a catwalker to prove me wrong.

PHASE 2: THE EARLY SKIRMISHES

Without diminishing the romance, I think it's good to approach the early stages of relationships as a classic military campaign. Reading *The Art of War* is probably much more useful than *Cosmo* at the beginning. Getting yourself into the power position is critical – the same as claiming the top of the hill in a battle. There are as many ways of getting there as there are ways to win a war: how quickly you text or call back; how available you are; and how many friends you have of the opposite sex. The importance of winning this stage of the game, as with all relationships (be it with women or horses), is that you establish that you hold the whip. If you find yourself on the losing end of this particular skirmish, you've already lost the war. So, just be a good sport and enjoy the ride until you're put out to pasture.

Early encounters will tell you a lot of things about your date. For example, if the person in question tries to make you insanely jealous about their ex, lies to your face, rarely looks you in the eyes or constantly stands you up, they are probably the headfucker your friends warned you about. Steer well clear. On the other hand, if your new love tweets you manically, 'Likes' everything you post on Facebook or pops up in places you wouldn't expect them to be, conclude quickly that you have met a rabidly insecure stalker. In both cases, pack up your toothbrush, hide the pet rabbit and break things off as quickly as possible. Remember to delete them from your contacts and block them from all social media interactions.

> You're sweet, but friending my entire family on Facebook is worryingly premature considering we only met last week. It's been fun but your contract is terminated.

THE DATING GAME

PHASE 3: THE STEADY STAGE

DON'T STICK AT THIS STAGE FOR TOO LONG UNLESS YOU REALLY HAVE FOUND THE ONE (SEE 'WHAT TO LOOK FOR IN A BUSINESS PARTNER').

Long-term relationships can get in the way of all sorts of things and if your partner doesn't push you to reach your full potential, then you can become complacent and waste time. A relationship where you aren't being pushed is like a really comfortable pillow, you will sleep really well but you will also find it harder to get out of bed in the morning.

PHASE 4: BREAKING UP

WHEN IT'S TIME TO GO YOUR SEPARATE WAYS, ALWAYS GIVE A BREAK-UP GIFT EXTRAVAGANT ENOUGH TO REFLECT THE AMOUNT OF TIME YOU SPENT TOGETHER.

- One night: cab fare
- One month: £10 WHSmith's voucher
- Six months: solo ticket to a West End musical – better they start enjoying their own company now
- One year: one-way ticket to a place you've never been ... and will never go

'A BREAK-UP SHOULD BE A MUTUALLY MOTIVATIONAL EXPERIENCE'

BOULLE'S WOOING WAYS

WHEN IT COMES TO AFFAIRS OF THE HEART, DON'T GO FOR THE OBVIOUS MOVE. DOUSING HER IN DIAMONDS ONLY WORKS FOR SO LONG — I SPEAK FROM EXPERIENCE. WHEN THE DAZZLING DIAMONDS BECOME DOWNRIGHT DULL, USE SOME OF MY TRIED-AND-TESTED TECHNIQUES TO GUARANTEE YOU DELIVER A 'BOULLIN' TIME, EVERY TIME.

BOULLE'S WOOING WAYS
HOW TO WIN AT DATING

1 Set up a romantic picnic in the park, complete with hamper, champagne, strawberries, the works. Just remember to kindly ask the nearby vagrant to give you some *alone time*.

2 A personal favourite is the backwards date. Start with what you would finish with, and finish with what you start with – well, you get the idea.

3 Spend a night in the garden in your very own cardboard fort, built by your very own hands and lit with fairy lights. Girls dig a handy man. Turrets go the extra mile. I actually really enjoy these dates – I *am* King of the Castle, after all.

4 Depending on where you want this relationship to go: kidnap her. Let's try and keep this friendly, so best leave out the ski masks and duct tape. Unless you're into that sort of thing.

5 Role playing: go to Ikea, and in each of the display rooms act out a different scene. For example, if there were to be a fake fireplace and books, you could 'pretend' to be a boring couple reading in front of the fire. Be careful, it might feel a bit like you're acting out the future and she could leg it ... or worse, enjoy it.

6 Any average date + blindfold = good times.

7 Go to the local animal shelter and play with the puppies and kittens – so she can see you have a sensitive side. Make sure it's clear that you will *not* be taking one home. Pedigree or nothing.

8 Rent ridiculous, but mildly believable, costumes – moustaches, crazy hair, etc. Put on accents and go to a very nice restaurant. Do not break character until the morning after.

9 With all these vampire films and TV series there is bound to be an entire generation of girls with vampire fetishes, so take heed. Tell her to bring her passport, whisk her off in the private jet to a decrepit Romanian castle for a candle-lit dinner with plenty of Red. If you get the right vibes, go for a cheeky bite. Definitely a situation you want to gauge correctly though.

10 If you are so head over heels that she makes you want to write poetry – do it! It worked for Wills Shakespeare, Pablo Neruda and, my personal fave, Robert Herrick. He clearly had game.

WARNING: *These suggestions come with the distinct stamp of The School of Boulle. I cannot be held responsible for any slaps or thrown drinks.*

BOULLE'S JEWELS

WHAT THE STONE IN YOUR ENGAGEMENT RING TELLS YOU ABOUT YOUR RELATIONSHIP

DIAMOND
Every engagement ring should have at least one diamond or there is something very wrong – with the ring *and* the relationship.

RUBY
Be very careful if you give a girl a ruby. It's said that it encourages ambition and thirst for power. Possibly bad in a relationship, unless you're into that sort of thing.

EMERALD
Meant to stand for enduring love. That's pretty good. I think if someone gives you an emerald you can invest in adjacent cemetery plots.

OF ENGAGEMENT

BLACK OPAL

If your beloved presents you with one of these, look him in the eye and ask for a prenup, because this marriage is going straight to the lawyers.

JADEITE

If you get an engagement ring with jadeite, run to the nearest pawnbrokers, sell it and run away with the proceeds. The world's most expensive gem is too good for anyone's finger.

JADE

A bit common. Has about as much class as a glacé cherry.

CUBIC ZIRCONIA

Whilst this is clearly a calculated hedge on the man's part, girls take note. If he doesn't pony up before you say 'I do', better say, 'I don't'.

THINK YOU'VE FOUND 'THE ONE'?

GIRLS, IF YOU CAN FIND A MAN WITH THESE ATTRIBUTES, HOLD ONTO HIM TIGHT:

- Industrious
- Inspiring
- Charismatic
- Good looking
- Great taste in clothes
- Well connected
- Well travelled
- Poet
- Knows how to handle a horse
- Animal rescuer
- Auburn
- Libra
- Six foot
- Entrepreneur

I ♥ U

GUYS, FROM MY EXPERIENCE AND OBSERVATION OF RELATIONSHIPS, IF YOU CAN FIND A GIRL WITH THE FOLLOWING QUALITIES, IT MAY BE TIME TO TRADE IN THE PORSCHE FOR A VOLVO ESTATE:

- Good skin and bone structure (think of the offspring)
- Warm and loving personality
- Educated
- Pliable
- Supple
- Tall-ish
- Active
- Good-looking friends (always hedge)
- Advanced secretarial and culinary skills
- Horsey
- A title
- A lover of animals
- Charitable (working in an orphanage in her gap year is sufficient)

HEIR AFFAIRS

**KIDS ARE AN INVESTMENT:
NURTURE THEM WISELY AND
THEY'LL PAY DIVIDENDS LONG
AFTER YOU'VE STOPPED
THEIR ALLOWANCE.**

HEIR AFFAIRS

WHEN TO HAVE THEM

Don't have children until you've got some money in the bank. If you have them at 35, you'll be 55, fat and rich by the time they're 20. They will thank you.

GETTING THEM STARTED

As well as a good school, your responsibility lies in giving them just enough lovely lucre to get started, but not so much that they don't feel the need to achieve anything. Always make sure that your children pay their way. Setting them revenue targets for each school year so that they contribute to the fees is good business practice. Never over-indulge them.

PARENTS' FINANCIAL EXPOSURE CALCULATION

$$\left[\{A \times 18\} \mid (B/100)\right] \times \left[C - D - E\right] = \left[G\right]$$

Annual sum to be spent on child from birth to eighteen [A] divided by family wealth [B] divided by 100 multiplied by the school fees [C] less interest [D] and less child's annual contribution accrued [E] equals the net drain on your resources [G].

HEIR AFFAIRS

NAMING YOUR CHILDREN

A name often defines a person's character. A 'Charlotte' is bound to be more literary than a 'Chardonnay'. Go for names that will help your child in the future. Apparently, naming your child Laura or Lawrence will more likely produce a lawyer, for example. So choose carefully.

Go for strong names – Balthazar, Boris or Adonis – but hedge with a neutral middle name (like Oliver, Charles or Sebastian) in case they turn out to be decidedly better off in the slow lane. Then at least they can gear down.

It's important to be aware of the rhythm of the name. If your surname has just one syllable, avoid a single-syllable forename (Hank Boulle just wouldn't work). Avoid rhyming names; nothing good came from Hannah Montana or Jacques Chirac (Evel Knievel is the one notable exception).

Finally, remember that if you name them properly, you're doing them a favour for which they will be grateful for the rest of their lives. They may even refrain from putting you in the nursing home before you start dribbling and perhaps allow you to visit their children once in a while.

THE
BRO
CODE

BUSINESS AND ROMANTIC RELATIONSHIPS COME AND GO, BUT YOUR CLOSE FRIENDSHIPS ARE LIFE-LONG, AND SHOULD BE REVERED. FOLLOW THE FIVE SIMPLE RULES OF THE BRO CODE TO ENSURE YOU STAY FRIENDS FOREVER.

1 Always look after your bros: 'I'm your tortilla, dude, I've got you covered.'

2 Never go after your mate's ex-girlfriend (or current girlfriend, for that matter), but if you can't control yourself then ask permission first. It's a respect thing.

3 Tell it like it is – lying is for poker.

4 If a friend gets screwed over: first comfort him with beer; then play pranks on him (see PRANKING PRACTICALITIES, p85) to take his mind off the whole ghastly business.

5 Do your friend's PR for them. When meeting mutual acquaintances highlight the qualities which make them your bro – they'll be sure to return the favour.

SOCIAL MEDIA

Twitter is my preferred method of networking socially. The 140-character limit means you can tweet your tidings to the world, yet still have time to go out and live your life as well. Some advice for tweeting:

- Tweet interesting or unusual things like your 'out-for-the-count' housemate using the litter box as a pillow.

- Do be original and always try to be funny. But if you're not funny, just respond to funny people. You'll seem funny by association.

- Tweet enough, but not too much. Anything more than once an hour makes you look like a twaddict.

- Don't be vulgar, bitchy or racist. But do be a Good Samaritan and help out Alan Sugar with his grammar from time to time.

- Don't use textspeak on Twitter – unlss u rn out of chrctrs.

Hit me up:
@FrancisBoulle
#Boullesjewels

LIFE'S LITTLE NO-NOS

- Dressing your pets as people – they are powerless to comment on your fashion sense
- Wearing high heels on a yacht or a bouncy castle
- Driving your own Rolls-Royce
- Smoking around children
- Being indiscreet about yourself or others – gossip is pretty rank
- Cruelty to animals
- Releasing your own sex tape, or your ex's
- Plastic surgery – you're beautiful just the way you are
- Being rude to staff – yours or someone else's
- Judging people – not everyone has had the same opportunities you've had
- Being a stingy tipper
- Accepting a peerage when you don't deserve it
- Being an eco-slob – do your part, dude

PRANKING PRACTICALITIES

LIFE CAN'T BE ALL BUSINESS, WE ALL NEED A RELEASE FROM THE STRESSES AND STRAINS OF EXISTENCE. THERE'S NOTHING BETTER THAN A GOOD PRANK TO KEEP THE SPIRITS UP. BE AS CREATIVE AND CLEVER AS POSSIBLE, BUT BE SURE TO OBSERVE THE FOLLOWING RULES TO AVOID A PRANK GETTING OUT OF HAND. ☛

PRANKING PRACTICALITIES

- A prank is, by necessity, at the expense of someone else. Avoid physical harm – there's an un-crossable line between pranking and bullying (or breaking the law). Pranks should be harmless and humorous, even to the person being pranked.

- Never vandalise – it's just not done, a bit like bullying an object.

- If you're still at school, it's the perfect pranking ground – I don't endorse this, but if you must do it, for God's sake, don't get yourself expelled. Be creative, not an idiot.

IF YOU'RE PRANKED YOURSELF – BE A GOOD SPORT; IT'LL REDUCE THE CHANCES OF BEING PRANKED AGAIN AND YOU'LL BE ABLE TO SURPRISE THE PRANKSTER WHEN YOU GET YOUR REVENGE (SEE P88).

HILARIOUS :-)

NOT SO HILARIOUS :-(

Faking a teacher kidnap in a school lesson (as long as the teacher is in on it) ➤ Kidnapping your teacher for real (definitely illegal, too)

Filling a room full of balloons so it's impossible to get in ➤ Filling the room full of balloons while you're still in it (pretty dim)

Putting your hands in front of a friend's face and saying, 'Guess who?' while an accomplice pours an entire salt shaker in their coffee ➤ Putting anything other than salt in their coffee

Dismantling your teacher's car and reassembling it in the school library ➤ Forgetting how to put it back together again

Pretending to drive off as you pick someone up ➤ Actually driving off

Wrapping your passed-out housemate in tin foil and then waking him up by screaming, 'Oh my God, where did they take you?' ➤ No, that's just hilarious

GETTING EVEN*

IF YOU'VE BEEN WRONGED YOU SHOULD ALWAYS GIVE THE PERPETRATOR THE CHANCE TO MAKE AMENDS.

IF HE OR SHE DOESN'T, THEN IT'S TIME TO START PLOTTING...

Here are some general observations on how to extract the most effective payback (and see PRANKING PRACTICALITIES, p85, for suggestions of creative vengeance – best executed amongst friends).

- Always bide your time. Let the memory of the offence fade in the mind of your victim and then strike with your most effective plan – they will have no idea why it happened.
- Never do anything that's physically dangerous – cutting brake cables is just bad form.
- On the other hand, subscribing them to a latex lovers' magazine using their work address is always a winner.
- Stealing someone's clothes when they're in the shower.
- Changing someone's name to Prince Pansy Pants or Lascivious Lolita by deed poll without their knowledge (see THE BOULLEIAN LIBRARY, p128).
- Swapping mobile numbers on someone's phone so they start sexting their mother or grandmother, rather than their girlfriend or boyfriend.
- Signing someone up to a dating website and writing a 'creative' profile for them.

* DISCLAIMER: *The author accepts no liability for the content of this page or for the consequences of any actions taken on the basis of the information provided. Furthermore, he is innocent of all charges of notorious vengeful acts that have been alleged to have been committed by him. He didn't do it. Whatever it was. 'Francis Boulle is innocent.'*

EDITOR'S NOTE: *As is the publisher! Thank God for indemnity clauses…*

'WHEN I'M TRYING TO DEAL WITH BETRAYAL I TRY TO THINK WHAT JESUS WOULD DO. JESUS IS LIKE A KIND OF SUPERHERO, YOU KNOW, HE GOT SHIT DONE'

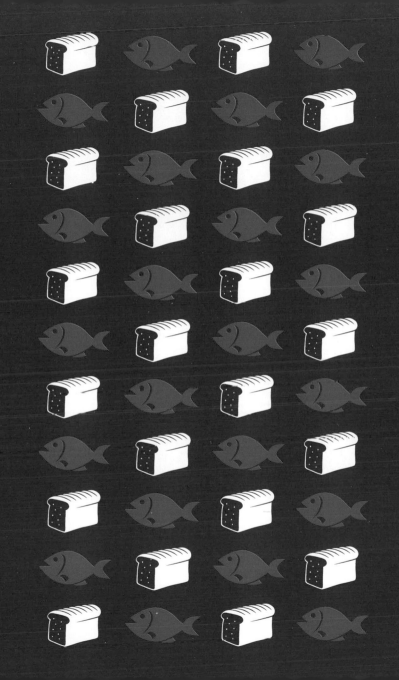

SW1 SLANG

HERE'S A QUICK GUIDE TO MY FAVOURITE AND MOST USEFUL EXPRESSIONS: I WANT ONE OF THEM TO CATCH FIRE ON TWITTER – USE #BOULLESJEWELS TO TELL ME YOUR FAVOURITE.

Chief, *n.* A loser. 'He's a total chief.' Originates from Eton.

Chin, *n.* A chinless wonder; somebody who always wears tweed and bright-coloured trousers, and aspires to live in SW1.

Cock-block, *n.* When a third party intervenes to stop two people having sex.

Coincimental, *adj.* When something is so coincidental, it's mental.

Dust, *vb.* To depart. 'He downed his espresso and dusted.'

Dutty wine, *n.* A dance performed on your head. Best done on a beach, preferably in Barbados.

Figjam, *n.* A person with a 'Fuck Me I'm So Great Just Look At Me' attitude.

FOMO, *acronym* Fear of missing out.

Goive, *interj.* Expresses a general disinterest in one's situation or surroundings. 'You're going to be late for Latin prep.' – 'Goive.' Originates from Winchester College.

Image, *adj.* When a person exhibits behaviour simply in order to gain attention. 'That's so image.'

Liming, *vb.* Hanging out on the beach (usually before showing off my dutty wine).

Low, *adj.* Incredibly uncool. 'His girlfriend caught him with her sister, very low behaviour.'

Meat, *n.* Lets someone know that their joke wasn't funny. 'And so the penguin never recovered.' – 'Meat.'

Picnique electronique, *n.* Having a picnic with accompanying pumping electro music (see FESTIBOULLES, p132).

PLUs, *acronym* 'People Like Us': 'It's a nice pub, full of PLUs.'

Prep school, *adj.* Engaging in behaviour that would typically be seen on a prep school playground. Like asking a friend to find out if someone likes you.

Rinse, *vb.* To put someone down, brutally.

Saucisson, *n.* Expresses distrust in the truth of someone's claim. Accompanied by a hand gesture in which the little finger and thumb are splayed out and the hand is shaken. 'It's totally in the bag.' – 'Saucisson.'

Savage, *adj.* Expresses an empathetic understanding of how bad a situation is for someone: 'I got to bed at six, but had to get into work by eight.' – 'Savage.'

Schnoot, *n.* A cigarette: 'Pass me that schnoot.'

Schoolboy, *adj.* Schoolboy error, making a mistake when you really should know better.

Schweff, *n.* Someone who spends 90 percent of their time trying to get action, even at the expense of their friends.

Shark, *vb.* To pursue someone aggressively. Often said of men who are after women.

Shred, *vb.* Generally doing things well. 'Man, I am a natural-born shredder.'

Soak, *n.* A lie-in.

Village, *adj.* Average, provincial. 'Mate, that's so village.'

**IT'S ALL ABOUT
FINDING THE
OPTIMUM PATH
TO THE TOP**

SPORT AND SPORTSMANSHIP

SPORT IS AN INTEGRAL PART OF ANY GENTLEMAN'S LIFE. NOT SIMPLY PLAYING EXISTING SPORTS, BUT ALSO INVENTING NEW ONES. IT IS AN ACTIVITY AT WHICH THE ENGLISH EXCEL.

SPORT AND SPORTSMANSHIP

ONE OF THE SPORTS I INVENTED AND PLAYED COMPETITIVELY THROUGHOUT MY SCHOOL DAYS IS 'APPLE'.

To play the game one needs an apple and some opponents. Best played on a clay court, the apple is thrown around amongst the players until it is dropped. The person who drops the apple has to take a bite and play restarts. This goes on *ad infinitum* until the apple is no longer. Whoever has the last bite loses because he has to eat a very dirty bit of apple.

Get out there, be creative and invent your own sport. Let me know what you come up with. We might just make a business out of it.

HERE ARE MY TOP TEN SPORTS TO GET THE ATHLETIC JUICES FLOWING:

- Hawking, preferably in the country. Sloane Square Shih Tzus are an endangered species, apparently.
- Boar throwing, Forest of Fontainebleau. Heavy, hairy and ornery. Be prepared to leg it and possibly die. They have amazing stamina and can chase you for miles. Just ask my father.
- Jousting, in a supermarket atop thine trolley steed. Jokeys.
- Fencing, Lansdowne Club. For if you lose the joust.
- Catapulting, anywhere devoid of people and animals. Play nice and aim for the apples, not the birds.
- Real tennis, the Oratory School, Radley or Hampton Court Palace. I'll see you there. Game on.
- Buzkashi, the Afghan national sport. Similar to polo but instead of mallets and balls simply a headless goat. I'm serious.
- Underwater rugby, played with a weighted ball and two underwater baskets as goals. Great for fitness. Non-smokers only.
- Winter water pistols at dawn, Thames towpath. Super Soakers and T-shirts ... ladies ;-)
- Sprite stalking, Scottish Highlands. Bring your night goggles and waders. The little tykes will take a chunk out of your ankles.

SKATEBOARDING:
THE MOST ZEN OF BOARD SPORTS

I've been fearlessly riding the world waves on a board, since I took the shaft and handles off a scooter to make my first skateboard at the age of six. Never looked back. For me, skateboarding has always been not only an enjoyable means of transport, but also a righteously Zen activity. Nirvana on a board. If you want to chase the same high, make sure you pick a skateboard that is right for your size, weight and level. First, you need to work out if you're 'goofy' or 'regular' footed. If you're goofy – like me – then your left foot steers the board and your right foot goes at the front. If you're regular, it's the reverse.

BE WARNED: *Old people and dogs have something against skateboarders – best to steer clear of both.*

'YOUTHS SHOULD
BE ENCOURAGED
TO SKATEBOARD...

...IT'S CATHARTIC AND WILL STOP THEM STABBING EACH OTHER'

THE SURFING SEASON

WHEN NEWQUAY IS RAMMED AND YOU WANT TO GET AWAY FROM THE WAXBOYS, CHECK THIS SURFING CALENDAR AND GO DEEP WITH YOUR BROHAHS.

MAY: Head for Anakao, Madagascar. If there's a southern swell, swick long barrels on a reef brake await the experienced surfer, but watch out – crystal-clear water.

JULY: Cap-Ferret or Lacanau are perfect. Approach from Bordeaux, and slink through a nudist beach to get to the waves. German girls are particularly friendly here. Schwinga swoosh! (Not sure what that means but I like the sound of it.)

SEPTEMBER: It must be J-bay – Jeffreys Bay in South Africa – home to the Billabong Pro ASP World Tour. An amazing right-hand point break and sensational calamari. It's scoop. Avoid early mornings and evenings when the Men in Grey Suits (sharks) are scarfing most.

NOVEMBER: Cocoa Beach, Florida is the Big League. First Peak is a sacred beach for the dudes.

FOR THE WINTER MONTHS: You can't beat Kauai in Hawaii. Super point combinations on the western tip of the island. You'll need Big Kahunas to say 'Aloha' to these massive swells – like surfing, like life. Sha!

POLO: THE SPORT OF KINGS

Polo offers us a number of important life lessons about the way we conduct ourselves in business and in love. I'll leave you to ponder and apply them at will.

- The best polo ponies are descended from the Argentinean polo lines. Good breeding – selective breeding – is vital.
- The golden rule in polo is 'don't cross someone's line when they have right of way' – it's dangerous. Play fair and smart at all times.
- Ride your own mare. You'll get to know her better and become a better player as a result.
- Only the best stables will do for your bloodlines. Luxury, of course, and location, location, location!
- Always use the correct equipment – protection first!

'LET OTHER PEOPLE PLAY AT OTHER THINGS, FOR THE KING OF GAMES IS STILL THE GAME OF KINGS'

(Inscription on an ancient stone tablet next to a polo pitch in Pakistan)

BOULLE'S PARTY RULES

THROW AS MANY PARTIES AS YOU CAN AFFORD, IT POSITIONS YOU AT THE CENTRE OF YOUR EVER EXPANDING NETWORK. EVERYONE NEEDS A GATSBY IN THEIR LIFE.

☛

BOULLE'S PARTY RULES

DO:

- make sure when weeing into a bush that nobody is making out behind it – best advice my dad ever gave me
- provide or bring enough booze – bitter experience says there can never be enough booze
- try not to drink to the point of vomiting, but if you must, do so in private
- invite people you admire and would like to get to know better
- always have a marquee in case it rains – it *will* rain if you don't
- take the music seriously – hire a good Disc Jockey
- line your stomach first – no, not with alcohol
- always send a thank you note or text message

DON'T:

- try to hook up with the host's mother (or father or sister – at least, not in view)
- outstay your welcome ('what time is your train?'; 'have you forgotten your house keys?'; 'you look like you need sleep,' and similar enquiries are sure signs you've outlived the party – go home)
- take pictures of everything – live a little and leave the obsessive chronicling to the Facebookers
- spray-paint your host's house – it's not very polite
- block the loo

BOULLE'S PARTY RULES

ICEBREAKERS

Icebreakers can be tragic, and should only be attempted by experts or the result may be party permafrost. These usually work for me:

- Encourage everyone into the pool: it spices things up and gives the party a more debauched and edgy vibe. Make sure you have sufficient floatation devices for the inebriated.
- 'Truth or Dare' always works: be sure to tell outrageous but somewhat plausible lies such as how you've recently discovered that you are the illegitimate son of Jackie Chan.
- Hold a Speed Dating session with a twist: everyone must pretend that they're the person sitting opposite them. It's more fun than it sounds.

THEMES

Try to be original when planning your party, avoid tired old themes like 'The 80s', 'School Disco' and 'Cross-Dressing' (incidentally, why do so many men like cross-dressing?). Having said that, you can never go far wrong with Bacchanalia and Toga parties.

Go for something more niche, like a Baby Bouncer party. Hire fit, rugger-type dudes, kit them out with adult-sized baby carriers, and strap yourself and your guests in. Guests direct their bouncer where they want to go. Remember to feed your bouncer.

'LOOS ARE THE CENTRE OF THE PARTY UNIVERSE – EVERYTHING GOOD AND BAD HAPPENS IN THEM'

WINING AND
DINING THE
BOULLE WAY

As you expand your network and surround yourself with successful and entertaining people, one of the most critical and rewarding skills to develop is the ability to entertain well, either at home or out. Knowing your way around a wine list is essential. Understanding the difference between well-dressed microwave meals and authentically delectable dishes will keep you in demand as the host with the most.

When dining at home, construct the menu as carefully as the guest list. It should be something you feel comfortable cooking, so always practise before the big night. Simplicity is more authentic, so don't overdo it. Go for flavour, quality, balance and presentation. Nobody likes a show-off, plus over-contrived menus just confuse everyone and make you look like a harried mess. Remember Bridget Jones and her Blue Soup.

It's not necessary to serve multiple courses to impress, but it is absolutely imperative that you serve a good wine that complements the food. Also, remember a simple meal can feel like a celebration with the right company and quaffable wine (or Jägerbombs if you can't be bothered with all of the above).

CUISINE

For dinner with your mates, you're safe making anything by Jamie Oliver. The man does simple, great food, which any reformed microwaver can manage. For something a bit more decadent, think Nigella Lawson or Jean-Christophe Novelli. (Women love Novelli's Mayfair eatery, Les Saveurs, and say anyone who can master his recipes will soon find themselves on the '100 Sexiest Men in the World' list. If it worked for him...)

BOULLE'S BOTTLE RULES

'LIFE IS TOO SHORT TO DRINK BAD WINE'

ANONYMOUS

WHITE: Go for Burgundies. You can never fail with a decent Meursault, Chassagne Montrachet, Puligny Montrachet or a good Chablis – Premier Cru of course.

RED: Meat and game dishes will appreciate a good Bordeaux – Chateau Margaux, St Emilion or Pauillac. Be adventurous and try out different wines and vintages. Just remember to avoid anything that pours from a box and you'll be fine.

CRÈME BOÛLLÉE

APPROACH THIS RECIPE LIKE A BUSINESS VENTURE. IT'S ALL ABOUT WHAT YOU CAN BRING TO THE TABLE. WHETHER YOU'RE TRADING DIAMONDS OR SERVING A FINE DESSERT, THE PRINCIPLES REMAIN THE SAME. MAKE SURE YOU HAVE THE INGREDIENTS NECESSARY FOR SUCCESS, AND THEN APPLY YOURSELF TO DEVELOPING THE PRODUCT BEFORE YOU PRESENT IT TO YOUR CUSTOMER BASE. THESE DECADENT LITTLE CUSTARD TREATS ARE EASY TO MAKE AND WILL ALWAYS GIVE A GOOD RETURN ON YOUR INVESTMENT.

SERVES 6 INGREDIENTS: 1 VANILLA POD | 500ML DOUBLE CREAM 6 FREE-RANGE EGG YOLKS | 100G CASTER SUGAR | EDIBLE GOLD LEAF, TO SERVE (THE DELECTABLE DIAMOND OF DESSERT DECORATION). YOU WILL ALSO NEED SIX RAMEKINS FOR SERVING

1. Preheat the oven to 150°C.
2. Split the vanilla pod in half lengthways, and scrape the seeds into a saucepan. Add the cream.
3. Heat the cream until it just reaches boiling point, then reduce the heat and simmer for five minutes – don't boil.
4. Beat the egg yolks and sugar in a heatproof bowl until pale and fluffy – like my main man, Boris Johnson.
5. Bring the cream back to boiling point, then whisk into the eggs until thickened.
6. Strain the custard mixture through a sieve into a jug or a bowl to remove the seeds, then pour into six ramekins so they are about two-thirds full. If you're using small ramekins, then you may need eight – use your judgment and be decisive.
7. Place the ramekins in a baking dish or a deep roasting tin, and then pour hot water around them to reach about halfway up.

8. Put the dish or tin on the centre shelf of the preheated oven and bake for about 45 minutes. You can make some important calls, set up a meeting or two, or send several emails while waiting. The custards should be just set but not firm all the way through.

9. Remove the ramekins from the tray and allow to cool, then chill until you want to serve them.

10. Sprinkle some caster sugar on top of each custard and then caramelise with a chef's blow-torch, or under the grill if you don't have one. This part is cool, but make sure you don't overheat, and mind your fingers. Leave for a couple of minutes, before topping with a piece of edible gold leaf and serving to inevitably impressed guests. Voilà – Crème Boûllée! *It's the business!*

MY ULTIMATE DINNER PARTY GUEST LIST

ALEXANDER THE GREAT THE MAN HELD HALF THE WORLD IN HIS HANDS. PROPS

AYN RAND AUTHOR OF ATLAS SHRUGGED. THE FUEL IN MY ENGINE

TONY ROBBINS A SELF-MADE TOUR DE FORCE I CAN RELATE TO

AMSCHEL ROTHSCHILD BANKING ROCK STAR

ELEANOR D'AQUITAINE
ONE OF THE MOST POWERFUL WOMEN OF THE MIDDLE AGES WITH AUDACITY I CAN ADMIRE

NICCOLÒ MACHIAVELLI
HAS SUFFERED FROM BAD PRESS – A TACTICAL GENIUS WHO TAUGHT MOST SUCCESSFUL BUSINESSMEN MORE THAN THEY LET ON

RICHARD BRANSON
THE MODERN ENTREPRENEUR'S ENTREPRENEUR

DANIEL LOEB
SURFING HEDGE-FUND HERO WHO MARRIED HIS YOGA TEACHER. NEED I SAY MORE?

J. D. ROCKEFELLER
HAS AN ASTEROID NAMED AFTER HIM

PICNIC PROTOCOL

ON THOSE DRY SUMMER DAYS, WHY NOT PACK UP THE CAR AND HEAD OUT TO THE COUNTRY OR TO THE NEAREST PARK WITH SOME FRIENDS, A PHOTOGENIC DOG AND A HAMPER?

WHAT GOES IN THE HAMPER?

Baguette, pâté, smoked salmon, oysters, truffles, foie gras, charcuterie, potted Stilton, Piccalilli, Dundee cake, fruit – including pineapple (not tinned), white wine (see BOULLE'S BOTTLE RULES, p118), Candy Kittens, plates, cutlery and glasses.

WHAT SHOULD ON NO ACCOUNT GO IN THE HAMPER:

Cheese squares or strings, crisps, lettuce, radishes, plastic or Styrofoam cups, recycled wooden cutlery, the photogenic dog.

IF YOU'RE IN LONDON, THESE ARE THE BEST PARKS FOR DINING AL FRESCO:

HYDE PARK: The King of Royal Parks – come through Queen's Gate, bear north and you should find some good spots.

KENSINGTON GARDENS: Elegant, good for skateboarding.

GREEN PARK: Peaceful and great for picnics, but watch out for joggers.

REGENT'S PARK: Henry VIII went hunting here before they built the zoo –the only place you'll find a rather satisfying 'inner circle'.

NOTE: *Picnics are not really a good occasion to conduct business – finger food makes for sticky keyboards, so leave the laptops behind and soak up the sun.*

BOULLE'S ANIMAL KINGDOM

WHERE ANIMALS ARE CONCERNED, I TAKE AFTER MY NAMESAKE, ST FRANCIS OF ASSISI. I AM ALWAYS LOOKING FOR ANIMALS TO RESCUE, WHETHER THEY NEED RESCUING OR NOT.

SIMPLY MUST-HAVE PETS:

HORSE: One of the best pets you can own but high-maintenance. The best things in my life happen when I'm on a horse.

RHODESIAN RIDGEBACK: Possibly the king of all dog breeds. Bred to hunt lions. The unsurpassed dog of my childhood (I miss you Cheshie, girl).

ST BERNARD: Respectable dog breed, if a little on the large size and a bit slobbery, but a pretty impressive pet statement.

LABRADOR: Agreeable and slightly dim. Adorable, and a good look for country picnics.

MONKEY: My father had a monkey in his twenties, and from the age of six I asked for one every Christmas. When it never arrived, I came to the sad conclusion that the old man at the North Pole was either not on my side, hated monkeys, or didn't exist.

CAT: I love cats. I fucking love cats. Do you hear me?

HIGH-MAINTENANCE BUT STILL AWESOME:

PARROT: Too bitey. They can be aggressive, loud and live too long. Birds of the feathered variety in general are best in the oven.

PILOT WHALE: Gentle creatures, but if they beach themselves they are a bitch to get back in the water.

POLAR BEAR: Cuddly exterior, but if they are hungry they *will* eat you, so probably best admired from afar. Cool fact: they cover their eyes up with their paws when they are hiding!

FALCON: Pretty awesome, but have been known to eat Shih Tzus in SW6.

BUDGIE: High turnover rate, which leaves one rather emotional.

THE BOULLEIAN LIBRARY

FEWER AND FEWER PEOPLE ARE READING ANYTHING OTHER THAN TEXT MESSAGES AND BALANCE SHEETS. **AND THIS BOOK, OF COURSE.** THANKFULLY I READ THESE CLASSICS WHILE AT SCHOOL AND THEY DELIVERED UNTO ME THE PRINCIPLES WHICH GUIDE MY VERY LIFE. THEY ARE DOPE. READ AND NEVER FORGET.

ATLAS SHRUGGED, AYN RAND: It's all about how the mind belongs to the individual, not the government. If you want to get to the heart of Boullosophy then read this.

THE GREAT GATSBY, F. SCOTT FITZGERALD: Set in America during prohibition. It's about appearances and things not being what they seem, old sport.

WAR AND PEACE, LEO TOLSTOY: Brilliantly riveting realism. I like to think of Count Nikolai Ilyich Rostova as my alter ego.

ANNA KARENINA, ALSO LEO TOLSTOY: 'Happy families are all alike; every unhappy family is unhappy in its own way.' Enough said.

THE PRINCE, MACHIAVELLI: 'One must be the lion and the fox simultaneously.'

THE SECRET DIARY OF ADRIAN MOLE AGED 13 ¾, SUE TOWNSEND: A must-read guide to teenage life – ignore the politics and remember what it was like to be spotty and morose. Not that I was ever either spotty or morose.

HARRY POTTER SERIES, J. K. ROWLING: This is what school should be like. I wish I'd gone to Hogwarts.

BUFFETOLOGY, WARREN BUFFETT: Brilliantly illustrates Buffett's value investment strategy. Buffett is on my 'would love to meet' list.

THE REPUBLIC, PLATO: Justice needs strong rulers, dude.

LOLITA, VLADIMIR NABOKOV: Riveting in its own way, but let's be honest, being obsessed with a twelve-year-old girl is not acceptable, unless you're a twelve year old.

THE OLD MAN AND THE SEA, ERNEST HEMINGWAY: The fishing tale to end all fishing tales. Watch out for the Noahs (Noah's ark = shark).

BOULLE'S JEWELS, FRANCIS BOULLE: Reading it means you are possessed of remarkably good taste and judgement.

BOULLE'S

FILM

CLUB

SOME OF MY FAVOURITE ALL-TIME CLASSICS:

FERRIS BUELLER'S DAY OFF: Taught me a very important life lesson about the importance of plausible deniability. People at school called me 'Ferris Boullé' so I suppose you can make of that what you will.

LESS THAN ZERO: Taught me early in life to steer clear of the crack pipe as things can go badly wrong. The book is also highly recommended.

THE BREAKFAST CLUB: More very important life lessons about not pre-judging others. We all bring different things to the Table of Life. Not to mention that Molly Ringwald is hot.

BACK TO THE FUTURE TRILOGY: I've watched these films hundreds of times, backwards and forwards. Time travel and DeLoreans are where it's at.

ST. ELMO'S FIRE: Never mind the shoulder pads, feel the friendship. Taught me the value of maintaining contact with buddies in my very own Brat Pack.

WITHNAIL AND I: One of the most quoted and quotable films ever. Good for drinking games. And firm young carrots…

POINT BREAK: Bank-robbing surfers and Keanu Reeves. Bitchin.

HARRY POTTER AND THE DEATHLY HALLOWS: Emma Watson's finest performance to date.

FESTIBOULLES

Summer is about fun, sun and hitting the festivals. It's also about rain, mud and trenchfoot. Regardless, you might find me at any one of these…

GLASTONBURY: Still the king and queen of all festivals. Boutique camping advised.

WILDERNESS: Secret forest parties led by a naked lady on a white horse. Talks by Arctic explorers – and me. Kid friendly.

SECRET GARDEN PARTY: Garden party gone mad. Think Alice In Wonderland. See you down the Rabbit Hole. Find me at the Pagoda.

WIRELESS FEST: On my doorstep practically. Love it.

BURNING MAN: Bring your own supplies, no money allowed. An intimidating thought!

SOUNDWAVES: Chilled beach fest in Croatia. Charter a yacht from Dubrovnik, anchor near the site. Potential interns swim over throughout proceedings. You'll probably be the only charter there – apart from me.

IGLOOFEST: Raving in igloos in Montreal. Best onesie competition. Chilly.

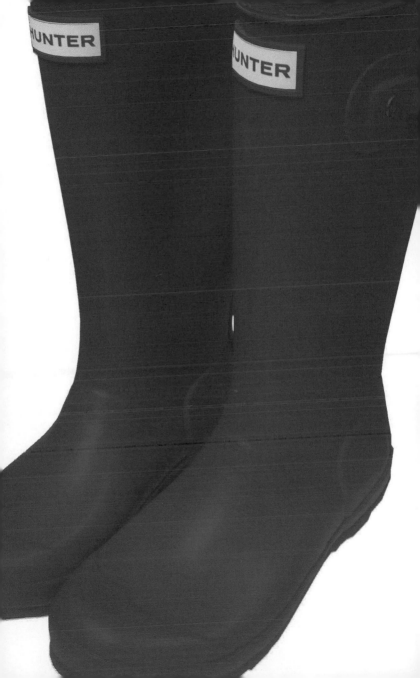

BOULLE'S

LONDON

A place to make things happen.

MOSCOW

Where much of London's money comes from. Be careful what you say – and to whom.

BUENOS AIRES

Beautiful people, beautiful horses, great parties, great polo.

CAPE TOWN

Great beach lifestyle and beautiful vineyards. Avoid taxis.

TOKYO

Invention and innovation, a neon nirvana where you can buy booze from vending machines.

PARIS

A great place to write poetry and find romance. Watch out for the Socialists – rampant at the moment.

BREAKS

HONG KONG

Manic, dirty, crowded, sweaty. Another great place to do business.

RIO DE JANEIRO

Where Rich meets Poor head on. Fascinating and lively. Carnival all year round. Notting Hill's older, more exciting sister.

NEW YORK

A great place to take the things you made happen.

NEW ORLEANS

The voodoo and party capital of America. Jazz, juleps and jiggery pokery abound in this Mardi Gras mecca. Purple, green and gold beads, the French Quarter currency, can buy you a whole new outlook on life. Laissez les bons temps rouler!

FEARLESS FRANCIS

COMING FROM A LONG LINE OF ADVENTURERS, I TRY TO PUSH MYSELF BEYOND MY COMFORT ZONE AT LEAST ONCE A QUARTER. THESE ARE NEXT ON MY TO DO LIST:

- Live a week of my life without touching the ground.
- Live and learn Kung-fu from the Shaolin monks for one year.
- Herd a flock of llamas through Machu Picchu.
- Be the first man to reach the North Pole with all of the Victoria's Secret angels.
- Spaceflight (Virgin Galactic).
- Rafting the White Nile, Uganda, with Gravity Adventures, SA.
- Disappear for at least a year with no explanation.
- Dress up bulls in suits and orchestrate a running of the bulls down Wall Street for poetic irony.
- Get a piggyback to the top of Everest.
- Spend six months trekking the Silk Road dressed only in silk.

TWEET ME YOUR OWN BOULLE ADVENTURE: #BOULLESJEWELS

BOULLE'S
BUCKET
LIST

- **MAKE BILLIONS (SECRETLY)** ☐
- **WIN THE QUEEN'S CUP POLO** ☐
- **TRAIN A HORSE TO WIN THE DERBY** ☐
- **DJ AT SPACE, IBIZA** ☐
- **HOOK UP WITH SOMEONE FROM A HARRY POTTER FILM** ☑
- **PLAY SESSION GUITAR FOR THE STROKES** ☐
- **PREDICT A STOCK MARKET CRASH (AND PROFIT FROM IT)** ☑
- **SURF PIPELINE** ☐
- **ADOPT A CAMBODIAN CHILD WITH ANGELINA JOLIE** ☐
- **STAGE A GLOBAL SCAVENGER HUNT FOR A DIAMOND** ☑
- **BEAT CHACE CRAWFORD AT STREETFIGHTER** ☑
- **PARTY WITH COURTNEY LOVE** ☑
- **PRESENT A UK VERSION OF** *THE DAILY SHOW* ☐
- **WAKE UP NEXT TO KATE MOSS** ☐
- **FLOAT A COMPANY ON THE NEW YORK STOCK EXCHANGE** ☐
- **HOOK UP WITH SOMEONE DRESSED AS CORN ON THE COB** ☑
- **CONQUER MOUNT FUJI** ☑
- **APPEAR ON LETTERMAN AND CONAN O'BRIEN** ☐
- **WRITE AN INTERNATIONAL BESTSELLER** ☑
- **NO MAN IS AN ISLAND. BUT I'D LIKE TO BUY ONE** ☐
- **BEAT GRACE JONES AND TOM HIDDLESTON AT TABLE TENNIS** ☑
- **HIRE WARREN BUFFETT AS MY FINANCIAL ADVISOR** ☐
- **BE DIRECTED BY SPIELBERG** ☑

iBoulle

Mellow and inspiring music
to write books by.

CYMANDE: 'BROTHERS ON THE SLIDE'

GOTYE: 'SOMEBODY I USED TO KNOW'

BONOBO: 'DAYS TO COME'

FRED PAGE: 'SMILES ELEVENS'

NUJABES: 'FEATHER'

SOULS OF MISCHIEF: '93 TO INFINITY'

ARTHUR BEATRICE: 'MIDLAND'

JEFFERSON AIRPLANE: 'WHITE RABBIT'

HONEYHONEY: 'ANGEL OF DEATH'

MADELINE PEYROUX: 'DANCE ME TO THE END OF LOVE'

ACKNOWLEDGEMENTS

AS ALTHEA GIBSON SO ACCURATELY NOTED, NO MATTER WHAT ACCOMPLISHMENTS YOU MAKE, YOU HAVE BEEN HELPED.

So in the spirit of gratitude, I would like to thank firstly my family, The Boulle Family Firm – all 100+ members and counting, my wonderful Aunt Cecile, my inspirational Bonne Maman, my American grandparents and family, my sisters, my father, and in particular my amazing mother who really has been there for me every step of the way.

A very big thank you to all of my friends. I love you guys, you know who you are.

Thank you also to Clive Dytor MC and Monsignor Anthony Conlon: a special thank you to you both for keeping me on the straight and narrow in my most formative years. Thank you to Mr Tomlinson, Snr., Mr Womersley, Mrs Nash, Mr Upton, my rowing coach Mr Fothergill, Barry Banks, Michael Roberts, Snr. (a brilliant legal mind), Chris Sayer, David Elliot (my Antwerp-based amigo), Fredrik and the Ferrier Family, Titus Roemer and family, Lord St Cyres, Rebecca Hoffnung, Lily Robinson, The Whitehall Family, Marten Collins, The Earl of Morton and the Douglas Family, Binfield Heath Polo Club, Hurtwood Park Polo Club, Knepp Castle Polo Club, the Lake Family, the Jackson Family, the Royal Family, Kanye West, The Prime Minister, Snoop Dogg (Lion), Bob Dylan...

I would also like to thank Chris Potts, David Grainger, Will Macdonald, Heidi Birkell, Alex Worral, Céin McGillicuddy, Sarah Dillistone, Daran Little, NBC Universal and Monkey Kingdom Productions, as well as Channel 4 and E4 and all of the crew and directors whose talent and professionalism make *Made in Chelsea* a pleasure to work on.

Last but by no means least, my Quercus Books family: the Toselands, and in particular my fairy god-publisher Jenny Heller and the irreplaceable Aunt Ione Walder, my editor extraordinaire!

Dedicated to my family,
past, present and future.

Quercus Editions Ltd
55 Baker Street
7th floor, South Block
London W1U 8EW

A catalogue record of this book is available from the British Library

ISBN 978 1 78087 921 5

2 4 6 8 10 9 7 5 3 1

Printed and bound in Portugal